RECENT PUBLICATIONS BY JOHN GREENING

The Giddings	(Mica Press, 2021)
Deer on the High Hills: Selected Poems of Iain Crichton Smith	(Carcanet, 2021)
Hollow Palaces: Country House Poems, with Kevin Gardner	(Liverpool, 2021)
a Post Card to, with Stuart Henson	(Red Squirrel Press, 2021)
Vapour Trails: Reviews and Essays on Poetry	(Shoestring, 2020)
Moments Musicaux	(Poetry Salzburg, 2020)
The Silence	(Carcanet, 2019)
Europa's Flight	(New Walk Editions, 2019)
Achill Island Tagebuch	(Redfoxpress, 2019)
Ten Poems about Sheds	(Candlestick, 2018)
Threading a Dream: a Poet on the Nile	(Gatehouse, 2017)
Selected Poems of Geoffrey Grigson	(Greenwich Exchange, 2017)
Heath, with Penelope Shuttle	(Nine Arches, 2016)
Nebamun's Tomb	(Rack Press, 2016)
Edmund Blunden's Undertones of War	(Oxford, 2015)
Accompanied Voices: Poets on Composers	(Boydell, 2015)
To the War Poets	(Carcanet, 2013)
Knot	(Worple Press, 2013)
Poetry Masterclass	(Greenwich Exchange, 2011)
Hunts: Poems 1979-2009	(Greenwich Exchange, 2009)

OMNISCIENCE

Greening

ISBN: 978-1-915079-25-1

Cover designed by Aaron Kent

Edited and typeset by Aaron Kent

Broken Sleep Books Ltd
Rhydwen,
Talgarreg,
SA44 4HB
Wales

Contents

Omniscience

John Greening

Red

Curiosity is lowered to the surface
and during those seven minutes of terror –
heatshield, parachute, hovering crane –
what rises from below is a sea of faces
for whom I had prepared a tennis ball
with papier-mâché, poster-painted it
crimson lake, adding icecaps
and Schiaparelli canals, but then forgot
(this was the time of the lost Mariners)
to take the planet out of my school bag.

1966/2012

Once and Future

Arthur C. Clarke, 1917-2008

That's him, crossing the night sky
above Manhattan, Sri Lanka, Borehamwood –
a UFO you might say, although

his own Third Law replies: *any*
sufficiently advanced technology
is indistinguishable from magic. The boy

from Bishops Lydeard (a Green Man puffs
his cheeks out in the church and Arthur sleeps
within the hill) held his breath beneath

home-made rockets, fireworks, until
he broke into the new millennium:
a sentinel, a spinning bone, a waltz.

*

We've lost our wise men, and are left with
the rich, who clamour like apes to be first
to climb the skies. We had dismissed it all

as science fiction until one day the moon
rocked our certainty, computers shrank
to the palm of a hand, and we held the world,

enthralled... which was when the virus wrote
its new version and the sea began to publish
our future. We cling on aboard a vessel

with no dialogue, only serious music
and a computer having a nervous breakdown.
He is safe, though, deep among the silver.

Omniscience

Science Fiction

*Mission*s, *The Martian* or *Lost in Space*,
while through the glass a yellow rose
called *Poet's Wife* is budding to the skies.

Empirical Science

For Stephen Hawking's memorial, a plaque
with his equation on it. Sir Isaac
knew enough to stay there in the dark.

Life Science

On the road to Huntingdon, we pass a dead
badger, two squirrels, a muntjac, the odd
pheasant, and... a rabbit? No, a leotard.

Exact Science

Putting up a shelf, for example, at a
certain point I'll see I could have done it better
using plumb line, spirit level, tape, etc.

Pseudo Science

Take steps, take note, take turmeric
with black pepper, steak with claret, smoke,
resist, pay, resist, jump in the lake.

Science Lesson

One master pulls at my hair and twists it hard.
Another draws relativity. A third
looks through me to see himself retired.

Forensic Science

We might have noticed it in the whorls
the forger left that clearly weren't from Arles
but we were hanging out with Gauguin and his girls.

Bad Science

Self-service checkout. Where's the slot
for the money? Where's the button for No? And what
the hell is a bagging area? Change? It appears not.

Pure Science

If you carpet your clachan with dead birds, you'll bewilder
yourself with dead babies, though you build
a hundred new churches on St Kilda.

Space Science

Thirty-five years in a mid-terrace groaning
with books and heavy with atmosphere, the Greening
family dream of space, are centrifuge training.

Science Kit

Fridays the grocer delivers a cardboard box
for me to convert to a robot that talks,
a computer, a rocket. My scissor hand still aches.

Sport Science

Conditions now favour the bowler. It swings
past barmy asteroids, through rings
of Stella, to where the final wicket hangs.

Medical Science

is what you leave your body to, so that when
they find this little rhyme-pump in your brain
they'll check if any poet has need of one.

Marine Science

As far from the sea as you can get, our field
where the glacier dropped its silt, rises, to hold
a wave there, a myth of the Flood unscrolled.

Social Science

Mass Observation. In this unmoving carriage
no one calls for a poem by Charles Madge,
Social Development Officer for Stevenage.

Science Correspondent

Since the entire Apollo programme is on your phone
and nobody can be bothered to look up at the moon,
it's no giant leap to say we might as well not have gone.

Political Science

Our Chief Political Editor declares
that a not very scientific poll now has
the situation much where it always was.

Colour Science

Erythrism is the official term
for the persistent feeling that the whole room
is smiling at your most revealing dream.

Music Science

With a single eyebrow to subdue and control
a resurrection, a revolution, a quarrel
at the Strausses, or a stubborn Viennese School.

Agricultural Science

Beyond *Farming Today*, can you hear
yesterday's plough horse, and our neighbour at its ear
whispering darkest Huntingdonshire?

Science Centre

His glasses gleam. He increases the dose, refuses
to accept he might be mistaken, uses
impenetrable language to bully the nurses.

Food Science

Cake plus cake over cake to the power cake
equals Brexit. If you then decide to take
the biscuit you may never get on your bike.

Environmental Science

A blandscape, someone called this – so much rape
and weedless wheat, so many fields without shape
or interest. One lark. No lapwings. A pigeon's clap.

Christian Science

Wasn't the Archbishop of Canterbury once in oil?
He'll know a thing or two about how to drill
carefully, persistently, so as not to raise hell.

Soil Science

From clay we come, as they say. Though in fact
I'm still very much alluvium, though I'll be packed
into the potter's field eventually, I expect.

Science Park

A godforsaken place on the outskirts of the city
where everything's efficient, nothing's dirty,
insulated from life, soul, and especially party.

Planetary Science

Mars was my obsession. I wrote the book
on Schiaparelli. Launched myself there, and took
the first step, even brought a gondola back.

Health Science

The thing sits under the hi-fi, a blue machine
with a tube that I'm supposed to plug in
and note the bloody level. No pressure, then.

Behavioural Science

He said you had to smack them, because
if you didn't, they'd be sent out of the class
to where the guy with the big stick was.

Natural Science

Surprising how people can't identify
the commonest trees. But then, I'd not even try
to say what make of car just passed me by.

Science Museum

I walk into Waitrose and *open sesame* –
Exhibition Road and please oh please let me
go through the magic door again, Mummy!

Gravitational Science

Did he eat them dipped in sugar, ruining his teeth,
then swing among the Bramleys? Planes leaving the Heath
defy the law that fell from this tree he sat beneath.

Nuclear Science

They wanted to bury the waste near Bunyan's village
where the tower (split from the church) keeps knowledge
of allegory to itself, and rings its own pilgrimage.

Domestic Science

A kitchen sink drama. The cat (to blame) just watches.
'Vinegar Tom', you say – that play about witches
by Churchill. We shall fight it without bleaches.

Veterinary Science

These days the cat sits happily on the mat:
perfectly aware it is a political parable, it
scratches desperately to go out, and yet...

Science Fair

What if Rosalind Franklin had paused to discover
the structure of male power, if Marie Curie had never
isolated Pierre, or Ada Lovelace only surfed for a lover?

Computer Science

Somebody in Oxbridge has their muzzle in a trough
supplied by a distant Tsar. Tell them to log off.
Tell them, Boris, it really isn't Godunov.

Economic Science

Rejecting your old coins like unacceptable words,
the car park machine spits out such duds
as crown or sovereign, farthings, groats.

Military Science

The drone that singles out a house, a room, a bed,
knows what you're up to more accurately than God,
and is quicker at numbering hairs on your head.

Psychological Science

The young are misbehaving in midsummer's urban void
while this old man drifts off with Jung on Freud,
a friendship which a single dream destroyed.

Science Prize

For the one who managed to levitate a frog.
For the one who saw the dinosaur in a chicken's walk.
For the one who analysed the personality of a rock.

Creation Science

When Eve remarked that something was making her
go pimply, Adam gave her the word cold, noting the core
of his own apple on their heaven's floor.

Rocket science

The stages fall away and I am left with this capsule
to take each morning. Getting older stops
all the magic, leaves us sitting by our toadstool.

Information Science

By being 'absolutely clear' and 'in no doubt',
they keep the code intact. No one can admit
to the tangle of roots that drives a green thought.

Junk Science

At the back of the shed you'll find the solution,
among those brackets and axles, pipes, machine
parts: a plastic bag, a hose, a sock will save the mission.

Science Lab

My mother sat in her white coat looking at smears.
Cancer wouldn't be her fate, though, no, hers
was to misdiagnose her footing on the stairs.

Biological Science

Somehow I avoided biology at school, sex
was kept for RE, though there were talks
containing forbidden words (though never fucks).

Brain Science

Haemorrhage? Still a word I cannot spell
since I heard it coagulate in my parents' hall
after the beat-beat of a small hours bell.

Geophysical Science

As Hardy might have said all those years after he and Emma
had hauled past so many striations – even firmer
than the principles of geology, love's little hammer.

Animal Science

The white tigers lie so beautifully in our zoo
and are the subject of much rigorous investigation too,
though we already know precisely what white tigers do.

Science Teacher

Write this down on your slates. Did you sharpen
your quill, your pencil? Replace that inkwell. You may open
fountain pens. Get a biro, can't you? Take out your iPhone.

Conscience

Now everything is simply reduced to a single
word which must trump all others, the angle
of a ray of light into a Hollywood jungle.

Prescience

Such as Kekulé's dream of a snake
biting its tail which gave him the molec-
ular structure of benzene. Call it luck.

Nescience

What we don't know is what we most need
to acknowledge, not to march ahead
shouting look what we found, look what we did.

Omniscience

After all, imagine what the past would make
of today, how much of this that we click
and swipe they could only understand as fake.

Barmouth, 1819

for Ruth Padel

Sea holly, sea rocket,
sea spurge, young Darwin
is botanizing in the dunes
of Merionethshire. While other
late Georgians step neatly
around the jellyfish, he prods
and flips them over hoping for any
promising beetles. All the dogs
return like comets when they scent
bones and a beagle in his dream:
it makes a moth-line for the hills
that captivate the town, barefaced
tellers of truth for how many
hundred million years to his ten.

Complex

in our Quaternary

                where even before

                                  poor Grandma

had been deposited

                in that place at Langley

                                  (clay

and silt)

        there were only

                      wind-blown

                                  brickearth

remains

        of sirens

                    tramlines

                                  a penny

turnstile

        a single erratic

                            like the Heston one

they spun

        into a sarsen

                      for the post-war Festival

of my sister's birth

                and a Comet

                            over London Clay

for me to spot –

        my father mowed

                      while my mother laid

crazy paving

        fifty million years ago

                        in my Palaeogene

the age of friends

who helped me dig

           that grave

                poor Grandpa

must have seen

      as a trench

           a better 'ole

                his battalion

might reappear from

        and not a location

              to shoot a schoolboy

rising up

     into my home-made

          horror movie

              down

through superficial

      deposits into

         unimaginably

            deep seas

Max & Min

At school we learnt
that an Ice Age
or Nuclear Winter
were on the way.
I was responsible

for the white louvred
box, observing
where its erratic
upright markers
had come to rest

after their glacial
ride on a flow
of silver through
the U-shaped
glass. How cold

it was, how hot
I noted down,
then with a magnet,
reset them, ready
for Climate Change.

Chemistry Lesson

First, draw a Bunsen burner,
showing how the inner blue
of the flame is hot and the
outer yellow cool, showing
the barrel or chimney, its
collar which will regulate
the flow, and this vital air
hole not to be confused with
that one where a rubber tube
hisses towards a stopcock.

Then, hand it in and wait for
fifty or sixty years, when
you'll begin to wonder why
it shows nothing of the man
who discovered a deep blue
poison in water, and an
antidote in rust, who's still
splitting light, showing us all
how if we'd only look up
we'd see what stars are made of.

Woolsthorpe

We have come to escape
the plague, much as he did
who lay in this orchard
and looked at an apple.

The walls of his manor
are kept tight by S's
whispering their master's
calculus to the air.

His leaden mask watched us
watch the video on
his life in our modern
coverings and mocked us,

making light of all our
efforts to concentrate,
the foolish way we split
him into the colour-

ful stories myth demands:
windmill, sundial, scratched wall,
this Maid of Kent, whose fall
raised laughter from him once.

Newton

Gravity

He did not discover it,
he proved it
           the tide
at Teddington Lock
recedes
         They said
you are a magician
Isaac
       the moon
over his mother's grave
at Colsterworth
draws closer
           No,
he'll not deny
the sun
       and respects
always the father's
absent authority

Optics

For two pounds a year
he has to be seen
to believe in the Trinity.

Time for a white lie
to be split into its
constituent parts.

A rainbow arches
from Lincolnshire
to the Mint.

Three Laws

That a fire in the laboratory
is never extinguished

That it is the error
unlocks the genius

That whoever pokes
a bodkin in their eye

sees best

Astronomer Royal

I observe the man –

he comes to the full
and his flaws show.

Sea of Unkindness.
Mount Arrogance.

In my star catalogue
his place is assured.

Ambitiosus.
Insidiosus.

But I am obliterated
from his universe.

Trinity Street

Outside the haunted house
crowds would hear
him as he passed: *meer
cheats and impostures!*

Back in his rooms, working,
he continued to ghost
any other scientist
who tried to get a look in.

Warden

The moon, uncounterfeited
as yet, saw how a dark glove

reached over to clip its edge
and scatter the silver, so

the stars came out. At Tyburn,
gravity claims another

coiner. At the Mint, Newton
has insisted on a raise.

King's Cross

The train at Platform One
is the 16.42
to Grantham

All about me
the world balances

The horse pulls against
the stone and the stone
pulls back

Epitaph

'...and All was *Light*.' My lightbulb starts to flicker.
His candle too. A message from the maker

to both of us that hiding at the back
there's something does not want to leave the dark?

Sir Isaac Newton Listens
to the Turangalîla-symphonie

One
A statue looks at a flower.
The statue has my death mask for a face.
Only the flower can think.

Two
I heard a glass harp
at the Royal Society.

Three
Contemplation of time:
different, successive
then simultaneous.

Four
Radiant blue.
My prism.

Five
The joy of the blood of the stars
will still be required to stream
in the firmament elliptically.

Six
An apple taking aim
at love's sleeping head.

Seven
Time turns on itself
like the nursery rhyme's
ten thousand.

Eight
Is a summons to
nothing?

Nine
Theatrical, theoretical
strings, but I am a ring
on a ribbon.

Ten
(Also a kind of
ingenious nonsense.)

Suspension
for J

Stepping on to it, unsure
quite when you came before

we talk of those many former lives
your hypnotherapist believes

may lie within us. Sceptical,
I walk while you describe it all

hanging above the Avon Gorge
half thinking of that other bridge,

the one you've dreamt of falling from,
but also of Brunel, the time

he took to build from here to there,
lacking the chains until that year

the necessary links were found
in one of his old bridges. A wind

catches us. But he was dead
and couldn't cross. Are you not scared

at what you're starting? And will you be
asleep or...? You're trying to convey

the process and we're halfway there
when three unheralded appear

in perfect silence, yellow vested,
fixing a link the years have rusted.

I want to know: if you should find
your lifetimes are not going to end,

forever struggling to refine
some fatal weakness in the chain

of birth and rebirth...? Our bridge swayed.
Don't look down. The other side

is near, you seem to say, suspend
your disbelief, and take my hand.

The Alchemist (Rilke)

With a disturbing smile, the lab technician
pushed back the smoky, halfway-settled flask.
He knew precisely now what he must risk
to raise the long revered archaic vision

within it. Epochs would be necessary,
millennia for him and for this pear glass
where it was brewing; in his own brain, stars
were needed, and in his consciousness, a sea.

It left that night, this horror he had willed
upon himself, he let it go. It turned
back to God and resumed its usual bounds.

But he, like a babbling drunkard, he sprawled
across that secret compartment, and yearned
for those gold crumbs he'd seen beneath his hands.

Alchemy

'And changing of some one syllable
May make this book unprofitable'
— Thomas Norton

Robert of Chester, fl.1140–1150

Under Spain's twenty-four carat sun,
he transmuted leaden Arabic.
So alchemy arrived in Europe.

Roger Bacon, c.1214–1292

Out there in the courtyard, look, holding
an astrolabe, waiting for the smoke
to clear from his new experiment.

Thomas Bungay, c.1214–1294

That experiment involved the two
friars blowing themselves up into
an Elizabethan comedy.

Sir George Ripley, c.1415–1490

Remembering what he'd learnt on Rhodes,
he took to the wheel, dreaming planets,
but was let down by his clapped-out verse.

Thomas Norton, c.1433–1513

The Mayor of Bristol had his L-plates
from Ripley: when the lights changed he knew
which lane was for gold, and which for God.

Thomas Charnock, c.1524–1581

> Long before Salisbury had heard of
> Novichok, he taught himself the dark
> art of manipulating agents.

William Holway, fl.1520

> At the dissolution, this Abbot
> hid his elixir in a wall, but
> neglected to note which (of many).

John Dee, 1527–1608

> Elizabeth's astrologer waits:
> a grimoire and a quick retort at
> the heart of the English Renaissance.

Sir Edward Kelley, 1555–1597

> Psychic, ready to scry. For forging
> gold coins, they had cropped his ears, but he
> could hear enough to talk with angels.

Mary Sidney, 1561–1621

> A lab of one's own? She managed it
> at Wilton, and negotiated
> the not-garden men prepared for her.

Robert Fludd, 1574–1637

> He only wanted to let the truth
> circulate, not for riches, but for
> planetary health, the elixir.

William Backhouse, 1593–1662

At sixty, he showed his pupil the
materia prima, but Ashmole
chose never to put it on display.

Sir Kenelm Digby, 1603–1665

There was the one about 'weapon salve',
reprinted twenty-nine times, then the
cookbook (try his viper-fed capons).

Sir Thomas Browne, 1605–1682

'With the dust of his alchemical
body' – skull gone, and these engraved words
stolen – 'he converts lead into gold'.

Elias Ashmole, 1617–1692

Out of the plague and the fire that took
the kernel of what he'd collected,
a husk survived: the Ashmolean.

Thomas Vaughan, 1621–1666

He and Rebecca did everything
Paracelsus advised, but nothing
could stop the couple dying of plague.

Sir Isaac Newton, 1642–1727

Knowing how the world went (round the sun),
he saw that it was advisable
to practise alchemy in secret.

J.P.Kellerman, 1779–18??

> Who, Googled, draws a blank, whose name has
> barely ever been set up in lead
> and won't be stamped on any medals.

Archibald Cockren, c.1880–1960

> Violent hissing, an explosion,
> and the scent of a June morning: he
> simply went on living in Eastbourne.

Bypass

'wasteful, weak, propitiatory flowers'

Bus to the hospital, but not to stay
this time, rather to head south

for the 'hills': across a roundabout, left
and down Worts' Causeway, just another

long straight suburban Cambridge street
unless you know about the keyhole in the hedge

that takes you through to a hawthorn-curtained path,
a milky way, pinned up, so the earth

can chant *till May be out.* Not normally
a beautiful place, our local author says,

and way too young. Today, however,
it draws me on and through like a piano roll

of Messiaenic birdsong, trying to clear
those other white rows, their frightening smell.

After

'that is a fairy story for
people afraid of the dark'
— Stephen Hawking

The fairies fill the night sky:
the men at long telescopes
tell their story.

But they have no other light
to read by, so they have
overlooked the books,

the countless books
of glimmering moment
and sharp experiment

that might have shown
what they would never
accept as they count

on fairies and live out
in darkness dustily
ever after.

Acknowledgements

'Complex' first appeared in the anthology, *Map* (Worple Press, 2015, ed.McKimm);'Bypass' was included in *The Hippocrates Book of the Heart* (The Hippocrates Press, 2017, ed.Hulse, French, Singer).

The epigraph to 'Bypass' comes from Philip Larkin's poem. 'The Building', which appears in *High Windows* (Faber & Faber, 1974).

LAY OUT YOUR UNREST

www.ingramcontent.com/pod-product-compliance
Lightning Source LLC
Chambersburg PA
CBHW031635040426

42452CB00007B/837